World Stage Press
Verse from the Village

Whispers & Conversations

Whispers & Conversations

POEMS BY RALONDA SIMMONS

World Stage Press
Verse from the Village

World Stage Press
Verse from the Village

Whispers & Conversations
© 2024 Ralonda Simmons
ISBN: 978-1-952952-66-1

First Edition, 2024

All rights reserved. No part of this publication may be reproduced, distributed, or transmitted in any form or by any means, including photocopying, recording, or other electronic or mechanical methods, without the prior written permission of the publisher, except in the case of brief quotations embodied in critical reviews and certain other noncommercial uses permitted by copyright law.

Printed in the United States of America

Edited by Ghislaine LeFranc & Ruddy Lopez
Cover Design by Jordin Kelsey & Emily Anne Evans
Layout Design by Emily Anne Evans

This book is dedicated to those it is meant to save and those whose hearts need mending.

Contents

Acknowledgments xiii
Preface xv

With Origins

A Blessing 5
Where's Home to Me? 6
Things Haven't Been the Same Since You Left 7
For Mama Shug 9
Egun Re O—An Offering 10
Daddy 11

With Spirit

H-Line Supernova 15
La Mère 17
A Buddha Begs for Sleep 18
The Listening 20
Can You Feel It? 21
Prayer 22
Laughter Is a Survival Tactic 23
The God in Me Thinks the God in You Must Have Gotten Lost
Somewhere 24

With the Intersection of Black and Woman

Be Like Black Girl 29
Chocolate 30
SBW 31
An Episode of Street Harassment 32

Brambles 33
　　Pretty 35

With Love

　　Some Hearts Are Way Stations 39
　　We Have Always Been 40
　　We Got 41
　　Princess Charming 42
　　3 A.M. 43
　　Malnourished 44
　　Carl Takes Dolly Out to Taco Bell in Their RV 45
　　Could Be 46
　　True Satisfaction 47
　　Summer '13 48
　　Haikus for an Ex-Lover 50
　　Doing Laundry 51

With America

　　Pre-K 55
　　Capitol 56
　　Black-Girl Blood 57
　　Dear Mother 58
　　Ode to the Mother of a Church Boy 60
　　On the Occasion of Robert E. Lee's Statue, Dismantled and Removed 131 Years Later 61
　　aka "Whose Streets? Our Streets!" 61
　　What Is America to Me? 63
　　Calling in Black 65

With Sadness

Birth 69

Resentment 71

S.A.D. 72

A Love Story 73

Pills 74

Insomnia 76

Geode 77

Divorce/Bankruptcy, Only $250 78

This Torn-Up Heart 79

With Poets from the Past

Reply to the Shepherd 83

I Do Not Believe in Heaven 84

Variation on a Theme for English B.(Or, First-World Problems) 85

Bodies 87

Dear Langston 88

Here's a Toast to Unknown Poets 91

Horror Show 93

III 94

I Want to Write a Poem 95

Out of Your Head 96

With the Past

Drapetomania 99

I Am Billie's Gardenia 100

Enlightenment 101

For Donny 103

'Trane and Duke 104

With the Body

Wildflower 107

Thighs 108

I, Too, Sing the Body Electric (Or, Lady Mag) 109

Shatter 110

Forgotten Rhythms 111

This Body 113

Commonalities 115

With Nature

Primavera 119

Earthworm Epiphany 120

Cataclysm 121

Recalling a Walk Through an Electrical Waste Yard in Ghana, in the Afternoon, Post-Warning 123

The Geology of It All 125

With My Higher Self

Nefertiti 129

Yellow, Forever 130

Maybelline 131

Woman 132

The Real Me, I've Found 133

It's Time You Spoke 134

Fury (For My Voice) 135

Pebbles 136

Fault Lines—Blessings to Self and Others 139

The Directive 140

Acknowledgments

My mama.

My grandmother.

All of my ancestors, known and unknown.

The English department at the Metropolitan State University of Denver.

Community Literature Initiative, and each of my fellow poets within it—thank you for sharpening me.

My cover designer, Jordin Kelsey.

My editor, Ghislaine LeFranc.

My layout designer, Emily Anne Evans.

The poetry community of Denver, Colorado.

Poetry for Personal Power.

Obatala.

And you, for reading.

Preface

Nothing happens without conversation. Worlds are built or destroyed on the understanding—or misunderstandings—between people in the space of the back-and-forth dance of communication.

At first, when collecting and writing these works, I struggled to find a common theme. Eventually, I realized that what linked each piece at its root was the fact that, within the space of each page rests a conversation, often between myself and some aspect of the world.

What you have in your hands is a culmination of more than twenty years of work. I have included pieces I developed as a young writer, as well as what has come from scholarly study, exposure, and a lot of love.

Each section is laid out thematically—I have done my best to coalesce my chaos into something that can be seen and felt. So, have a cup of tea and sit down. Let these poems whisper to you like an old friend.

Time to begin.

Whispers & Conversations

WITH *Origins*

A Blessing

Here we are, finally,
from these hands you birthed yourself,
gestated with time, attention,
with purpose, you stood up
in this world. I hope you ascend
to your highest vision, becoming what
those who have come before haven't yet.

I hope you fly to the side
of whoever needs you,
ready to soothe their pain,
able to highlight the connection
to their holy humanity, from yours.

I pray you save some lives,
pull somebody back from the ledge,
or better, prevent their feet from stepping
onto it in the first place.

I hope you still make your ancestors proud,
shining in their reincarnation,
continuing to link their chains and tears
to their liberation.

I pray you usher in a new day,
changing this world into something
much better than the one you inherited,
into which you came,
spreading light into any boardroom, courtroom,
statehouse, pulpit
you may find, waiting for a revolutionary
to open their hearts and ears
to your purpose, to feel a phrase
that further turns the world
and makes it more in line
with the vision God created.

Where's Home to Me?

Early memories depict sweet tea, sunsets, puhcahn,
brick red, back when I teethed the language
and tried on my granny's verbiage for size.
Learning to form my mouth around
an adapted tongue called less than.

I won't say I started from nothing—
more like Mississippi mud clay, a seed growing,
reaching up to the sky like a magnolia tree
in the face of history's beatdown,
oppressive like the sun, hugging me close
as a wet humid blanket.

I'm from here, like fried catfish, like not knowing
your place until it's time to be quiet.
Until it's time to move off the sidewalks
on the way to church, for your own good.

Luckily, I moved around—
back to my Inland Empire dreams,
full of dust, coughing on contempt,
obscured by smog. I still flowered,
despite my environment, despite expectations.

Clutched food stamps, stood in line for free lunch,
I couldn't get enough. Saw no beauty, not in myself.
It wasn't always looks.
My nose was always in books.

Back then, I was just taunted and...different.

My gaze wasn't my own at the time.
Where I'm from? I would say everywhere.
I can hold my own at any strange lunch table
or any school library, all for survival. And hey,
I won by learning to own it all, even the strange.

These days, I'm Mile High, and I smile wide
wearing my crown like the Queen of the Plains.

Things Haven't Been the Same Since You Left
Eulogy for a Hometown

Here lies the burial site of hundreds
of Saturday nights scented
by sweat, popcorn fumes,
and floor polish, haunted by
bygone laughter. Couples and singles skate,
contests and countless rounds
of the Chicken Dance, played
as loud and as fast as possible.
Now, flat and abandoned, the ashes
of everything long gone
        (Home hasn't been the same since you left)
wish they could have saved it, but if they couldn't save Carousel Mall,
Stardust didn't have a chance. Speaking of,
this is for the Montgomery Wards, who left first, followed by JCPenney's,
let the rest rot from the inside
until they dismantled everything
and left what remained to die.
They took down the carousel, threw away the little cobbler who sat for years,
faux hammering a nail into a shoe in the window by the door,
took apart the kiddie train we used to ride.
Remember that? Who knows where all the pieces are.
Now puddles sit where people used to walk.
Only ghosts live there now,
waiting for the walls to come down.
Remember driving downtown, waiting to see that clock?
You'd laugh every time you saw it because you knew it was your city's pride.
Remember that? Pride? Hasn't been the same since you last arrived.
You used to go with your grandpa to Seacombe Lake
(which was rough, even then) to feed the ducks bread and Velveeta.
He'd wrap the neon orange cubes in white bread
and you remember wondering why
and whether ducks even liked Velveeta,
but they gobbled it up every time.
How things change! Now, there's a wrought iron gate around the park,
and no one feeds the ducks anything anymore.

Speaking of parks, remember Perris Hill?
How you'd rush down the waterslide over
and over until it was time to leave—
That Inland Empire desert heat had nothing
on its waters. Now, tents sit like little hills
all over the fields. Kids don't play there either. Not like we used to, at least.
Everything is colored like sand. Everything dried up, set against smog and a
desert of dreams. I wouldn't dare ask you to come back because it's too late,
and being a savior probably isn't even your cup of tea.
I can't list all of our memories, and it leaves me bereft.
This here city, our hometown, hasn't been the same, since you left.

For Mama Shug

My Mama Shug
loved me like Sunday morning,
love's open-mouthed praise
between mahogany pews.
She loved me
like my tongue loved her cooking.
Like black-eyed peas,
fresh-picked greens,
like cornbread and buttermilk.
Like the heat that rose on her porch
every afternoon.
My Mama Shug loved me
like I was some miracle
she'd never seen.
Not yet some wisecracking alien
with knowledge beyond her years,
but a continuation of her own soul.
She loved me like syrupy-sweet morning heat,
bacon frying in cast iron,
eggs forming sunny-side up,
like butter and syrup
soaked into her biscuits.
She loved me like hallelujah—
I still love her like amen.
I think about her sometimes.
She sticks in my memory
like a shoe in Mississippi mud,
like a Sam Cooke melody.
I know she sent me these dreams.
Stuck in place like a Now and Later in my molar,
I hold her in my jawline
and I smile,
hoping every day
to make her proud.

Egun Re O—An Offering
Ancestors, Be Praised

Mine walked single-handed holding, afraid of what
they could not know, toward the shore, strong,
to meet the boats as they bobbed up and down.
They began to sing loudly, their freedom songs.

They set sail, prayed to God to return home
to their people, their customs, their mothers.
But the white men who held them threatened,
and they couldn't coordinate with the others.

Months-long journeys, glued close by sweat and shackle
to their neighbors, enemies, friends—abject misery,
without any food, drink, or human respect.
They laid there chained, and now we call this history.

Later, they reached the shore. In shackles,
marched through town, on the block they stood
to be examined and probed by rich or poor men,
found altogether strong, healthy, and good.

A bloody time, for years and years they suffered,
time spent starving, without personhood, all for free.
Who could have known, years later,
ten generations down the line, that would be me?

My ancestors, those who flew, those who sank,
those who fought—those who carried on and lived,
converged and made me everything I am today.
To them, all thanks, praise, and love I give.

Ashe.

Daddy

I looked for you in the faces of men,
in grains of sand. In clouds, I looked
for you then. But I don't have to look
for you now. Did you ever think of me,
Daddy?

Heard your voice today, not like I'd imagined.
Half of me smiled, half of me got angry.
Daddy, did you ever see me?
Did you ever dream of the woman I am
growing up to be?

I'd closed these holes in my heart forever,
in anticipation that I'd never
make your acquaintance nor survive
this semi-whole, halfway person.
Bastard Living, Sire, Daddy, Mon Père.
Did you ever care? Was I just an outline?
Was I? Or was I nothing at all in your mind?

I thought of you almost daily, driven crazy
with longing for what I thought I'd never have.
Daddy. 24 years since you were irresponsible.
Less six months, I drew breath.

This morning, I got closer
to putting that demon to rest.
Daddy.

WITH *Spirit*

H-Line Supernova

One late fall morning,
      I sat on the H Line train
    heading for Denver,
        my head full of worry
about past deeds and future failures,
    ears full of Coltrane's sax wailing
        notes to high heaven for his Love Supreme.
I peered out the window as the sun peeked
    from underneath the gloomy down comforter
    of cloudy morning,
        her rays reflected off the dark eyes
of office buildings sitting near the freeway,
    then bounced toward me.

        Suddenly, I had a vision.

I saw myself, outside of myself yet present,
    striding up the highest, greenest summit,
    staring the sun in all of her golden glory,
    right in her face.
I swallowed a ball of light that morning.
    Indeed,
        I took sunlight, high noon,
gathered it in my fingertips,

       rolled it around like a marble,

              molten,

       kneaded it like dough as more poured in—

I swallowed it, and it warmed me.

       It lit up the mold-grown dark places

where I kept decayed promises

       and dreams hidden, hoarded,

and delayed.

       Burned away, clear as day,

I knew then that I was a star

       swallowing a star,

       becoming unto myself

             a supernova.

                       I let the sunshine in and glowed—

                       everything was alight and all right.

       I opened my eyes. There, I sat and I smiled

             with a warm, full throat,

                  as John Coltrane exhaled

after playing his final

       note.

La Mère

How is it
that every time life
becomes hard,
I automatically yearn to go to the shores,
to watch waves come in
and go out dependably.

                                        This new world is unpredictable,
                                        just like all of the old new ones.

Yet the ocean remains
the same, its waters
departing and arriving
without fail. Rising
or lowering while trying
to reach the juicy fullness
of the moon.

                                        I yearn for the ocean
                                        like I yearn for a mother's hug
                                        after years of isolation.

Could it be because
the waters once held us,
incubating in ancestors' aspirations,
from single cell to simple form to tetrapod,
inching its way across and up
the shoreline,
burning its toes for the very first time?
And now, millions of years later,
                                    I yearn
to feel the hot sand between my toes,
pushing me back toward my mother
with outstretched arms.

A Buddha Begs for Sleep

If only I hadn't seen
what I saw one afternoon.

I had it good—
wanted for nothing except
something to do or see.
That day,

a sunny afternoon—
all the better to see
something that could
shake me out of my
complacency—a body
lying skin and bones
in the street.

                          And I haven't been able to sleep since.

Buddha. Related to bodhi—
the spontaneous wish
for the end of all suffering
on all planes of existence,
a seeming impossibility...

Until I searched far and wide,
but not before starving,
begging—to escape
the flesh of this world,
nirvana for all, a heady
dream. I wish for sleep.

Because my only qualification
was the ability to see.

Buddhas aren't supposed to wish for such things.
The purification process
was supposed to burn all of that
away. Or else I'm not who I say?
That's what my ego demands an answer for, anyway.

Perhaps I still have lifetimes to go—
spontaneous awakenings
heating me up until I burn away
everything that can't come
on this journey.

The thought makes me want to sit
with my back against a tree,
my only task to breathe,
to close my eyes to the illusion—
that's all, the better to see:
> A man lying bone-skinny in the street.
> A woman begging for some food to eat.
> A homeless child, dejectedly shuffling.

My eyes couldn't take all of the suffering.

                        All because I, not yet a Buddha, just had to see
                            and awaken—but now I dare not sleep.

The Listening

Like a lightning strike, the first time
I heard those voices, riding beats
like a Tilt-A-Whirl—the world slid sideways
as I pressed play. Heard the jazz
and the truth, measure by measure,
twisting words around notes like
pull 'n' peel Twizzlers, songs about change.
In myself, I felt the fissures. This heartbeat
in the same meter. This song
seemed to say everything that could ever
be said or had ever been. This poem
about love, about inner-city struggle,
boastful.
This song about love—this is a song
about love. Born from teenage daydreams,
just like the instrumentals and rhymes
I stumbled upon. That moment,
tunnel vision as I first got a taste of wordplay.
Pulled out dictionary, thesaurus, to find
and define words synonymous
with the bullshit I called life at the time.
Tools to hammer the pain into rhyme
and, at the same time, find melody in despair.
      And I don't stop, because I can't.

      And I won't stop, because hip-hop
      gave me the gift of my life.

When the sickness hits, I press play.
    Musical morphine speeds

        right to the pain. And I start to nodding,

                and I start to nodding,
                and I feel the healing.

And that... is the listening.

Can You Feel It?

At your best, you danced on water—
burst forth from the sky like first light,
glancing and reflecting, manifesting
this world, a creation myth.

The smile on your face was the sun—
we were your subjects, prisms
throwing the rainbows of your genius
far and wide.

Yes, you smiled with all peace and joy—
felt like the first springtime. You stomped
each step, throwing river-water raindrops,
sharing your joy with us all, kneeling
forward then standing upright, smiling.

Brought your hands high—
then clapped my joy into existence,
comets, and asteroids
shooting from your crown. I screamed yes
as you asked, "Can you feel it?"

Sprinkling stardust on my shoulders—
lifting rainbows over everything,
bringing color to a place full of rock
and sand, at least before you came.

So much light, we became one—
held hands in love, that current
sent from Most High to this earth.
With tears in my eyes, I became love
itself, and my heart no longer hurt.

Prayer

Dear God,

Been a while since my lips formed
to ferry words to your ears.
I guess somehow I was convinced
there was no way you'd hear the cursed words
of this lonely wanderer.

Arrogant to ask why—
why I was placed here of all places,
among unknown and hostile faces
with mockery on their tongues.

It's been so long, and Lord, I'm so lost.

Dear God,

I can see it in my mind's eye—
sitting backward on a ledge,
letting go and surrendering my life to you.
Don't know where I'd end up
and don't particularly care.
I just want the pain to end from being stuck here
alone, without a loved one
or a friend. I wonder who'd care.

Ceaseless wanderer, ingrate, wretch—
I look at myself and think: my existence
doesn't make any sense. Don't know why
I'm alive or if I should strive to survive.
I guess only you'd know.

I watch the skies darken. Ain't felt daylight
in about seven days. Guess you'll work
it out in your time. I just wonder if what you placed here
will manage to survive.

Laughter Is a Survival Tactic

An ancestral adaptation
passed down through generations.
I don't care if there's nothing to laugh at—
humor is the honey that leaks out
when combs pressed so flat,
their structure loses integrity.
The laughter, a sweetness
to make you forget about oppression
for just a little while.
And every second you wrench
from their bullshit is a victory,
sweet as collected pollen multiplied by time
and sunshine.
When the weight gets too heavy,
when death remains too real,
when there was no letup.
When the babies are hungry,
when they won't keep your name out they mouths,
when the news makes the winners losers,
and makes losers out of victims
with the reliability of a ticking clock…
Yeah, laughter becomes meditation
and medication,
an affirmation of inbreath-outbreath
when systemic neglect got its hands around your neck.
You damn right, finding some humor in the horror is superhuman.
A revolution in the lost breath, in the tears,
in the wit and agility passed down to me
through the years.
And now I sit with the benefit of ancestral wit.
I recognize I don't have to be sad about shit
because laughter is a survival mechanism in this world today.
The sweetest honey when all other hope has gone away.

The God in Me Thinks the God in You Must Have Gotten Lost Somewhere

Between your justifications of bloodshed,
finding reasons, manufacturing them
out of history's thin air.
You plank challenge, miming dead bodies.
You put black cloth on your heads,
black your teeth,
switch on your lights and water
in mockery of those who have none.

                                    The god in me wants to take
                                    the god in you outside to shoot
                                    the fair one—all hands, no nerve gas,

no knees, no threats,
no chokeholds, no handcuffs,
no rubber bullets, no tear gas.

                Nothing but air and opportunity, baby!

If the god in you weren't blind,
it would be just like looking in a mirror.
Instead, the scales of justification,
the need for status, survival, and god's favor
cover your eyes, and it makes me realize
that you must be deaf, too.

How can't you hear the cries
the bombs
the fires
the pleading
the planes
the planes
the fires
the panicked footfalls
the dying, the crying,

                                      the yelling—oh, God
                                              the yelling.

The god in you could do something about this.
Instead, your divinity covers its eyes,
covers its ears,
and yells so loudly over everything
that it cannot possibly hear—

                                        as I beg
                                   and as I plead
                    for you to actually see the god in you
                         to help you to see the god in me.

WITH *the Intersection of Black and Woman*

Be Like Black Girl

Be like Black girl,
not like that girl,
that girl with hips spread,
neck rolling.
Don't be too mad, Black girl.
Don't be too loud,
don't laugh.
It used to be against the law
for Black people to laugh,
to remind the listener
that she or he existed.
They desired silent shadows,
not flesh and blood.
Step out of line,
they will burn you
from the inside out.
Enflame you and say
you liked it hot,
hot as 1960s Philadelphia,
Mississippi.
We used to sing,
our movements tappin'
the ground like nickels
thrown against cement
with style,
with broad smiles,
tapping our way to freedom
undercover,
because our drums
rest at the bottom
of the Atlantic, playing
songs we can't hear.
But it sounds like waves
and blood pulsing
through our veins.
It's hard being silent
with forgotten gods
dancing in and around you,
begging for worship,
to scream their names in public.
Your mothers sit yelling
for you to say their names,
to never forget.
Just be like Black girl,
just like you already be.
Be yourself, Black girl,
for then you will be free.

Chocolate

Don't want to be your chocolate,
your caramel,
    your mocha mami,
    your devil's food fantasy.
I won't melt in your hand or your mouth,
    the taste of my sweet degradation on your treacherous tongue.
You will not cut into me as I scream.
    Not your birthday cake,
        not your hot-fudge sundae.
I am flesh,
    not a manifestation of guilt
        as you pack on the calories
that come from centuries of resource gluttony.
    No—don't want to be your brownie.
Not some passive, consumable sweet, no guilt trip.
If I must be taken, it will be on my own terms,
    not to save for later.
        If you must, eat me first.
    Don't hide your lips behind your hand in shame.
I am nothing to be ashamed of.
        Not your chocolate, crème brûlée, tiramisù human,
        not your dessert plate justification.
        Not yours. I'm not yours.

        I am not yours.

SBW

A safe Black woman is a
chalk outline, something not
experienced,
only sketched out
in popular imagination.

She's static, held in place by
history
and low expectations.

But what do you expect,
when you were supposed to die
years ago?
When your granny sat you at
her knee,
did she tell you to dream?

Or to lie still
as they mispronounce your
name
on purpose?

A safe Black woman
may be an oxymoron, a
paradox,
something truly unnamed,
not to be uttered.

Just keep your back strong—
don't drop that shit,
don't let them see
your light, not safe.
In these winds, you won't be
blown away.

A Black woman, safe?
Impossible, according to they.
But you know what I say?
Live brightly. Here's your
permission.

Gather the dust
you're left with, turn it to clay,
sculpt your best self, do all
except diminish
that light, Black
shine on sunlight,
magical, vibrant,
move in your awkward, human
ways. Shine

like the gold you are,
the star you are.

A safe Black woman
can undoubtedly exist in her
skin by focusing on the light
within.

An Episode of Street Harassment

"Hey, miss lady! You're sure lookin' good today
with that pretty dress on and those high-heels.
Where's your man? Does he hold you, pay your bills?
One taste of my love, girl, and you'll turn him away!"

"Ugh!" My walk speeds up and I shake my head.
Daddy said that's not how you talk to a lady.
I hurry past him as he hollers out, "Baby! Baby!"
He tries to make eye contact—I turn away instead.

How could she ignore me as if I was less than trash?
As if she was somehow better, maybe even a queen,
draggin' her robes. How could she be so mean?
How dare she, even if she does have a fat ass?

"Hey, bitch! I was tryin' to brighten your day.
I was just being nice. Your ass is ugly anyway!"

Brambles

You say it's just hair,
        not a battle to be fought and won.
A scar waiting to crust over because
        you won't let it close. An untamed jungle,
              you say, wild and confusing.
A tangled vine, ready to catch you up in its brambles.
        You say it's just hair,
not a crown of thorns
        tilted upon the head of the persecuted.
But this is my hair.
        My tangled thoughts not neglected,
these manifestations of ink and zinc and time
        not spent sitting in Sunday afternoon kitchens
with a hot comb to my kitchen,
        wrestling my follicles into a semblance of civility,
curled over and under in submission, bent
        and subdued
              because my halo of kinks was too much
for the uninitiated to handle.
        This is no petting zoo—
I didn't invite you into this midnight forest.
        There are no paths in this labyrinth for you to follow.
I know it's hard to swallow,
        this truth, coughed up, clog cleared
as if from a mane-choked drain.
        You say it's just hair. Historically,
        the cause of self-hatred and pain,
hidden meanings that cause confusion.
You say it's just hair,

        but I know better.
Crown of thorns no longer,
        these roses have bloomed into your worst nightmare—
        beautiful and irreverent.
My history, detangled with the conditioner of understanding,
        a wide-tooth comb through
              misconception.
My hair may be as soft as a lamb's,
        but don't get it twisted.
You say it's just hair.
        Are you kidding me?
I just shake my locs, evidence of divinity.

Pretty

I never knew what it was like to be pretty.
A delicate flower, so fragile
that to touch me would destroy my petals.
So delicate, the world would handle me
carefully
out of fear that, if I was ever destroyed,
all of the beauty would be sapped from existence.
      No—
I've never been that pretty.
I don't know what it's like to be morning dew
or a swan's neck.
I've no idea what it's like to be pretty.
All I know how to be is strong.
No time to sing these songs when I have to figure how to fly
on broken wings.
The world never seems to pity crows
but holds sparrows in high esteem.
Stroking the petals of a rose with reverence,
      never hesitating to destroy
what their eyes perceive
as a weed.
      No—
I've no idea what it's like to be pretty.
What's it like in that gilded cage?
Is it as cold in there as it is out here?
Tell me,
what's it like to be seen,
      to be considered,
      fawned over,
      taken care of,
          loved?
What's it like to be pretty?
I've plucked my brows,
hidden away unsavory parts of myself,
painted my nails,
spackled my face,

erased my hard edges
trying to fit in this place,
hit up sale after sale
trying to belong—
but to no avail.
Tell me, what's it like?
For I haven't the slightest clue.
To have teeth so white, the world at your feet,
prostrated in front of you,
untouched by a place so dirty, grimy, and gritty.
Tell me, if you can, what's it like to be so pretty?

WITH *Love*

Some Hearts Are Way Stations

Some hearts are way stations,
    closed Greyhound bus stops
    in two dirt-road towns after midnight—
    quiet, haunted, forgotten.

Some hearts are Grand Central stations,
    bustling and loud,
    cavernous, echoing all human life.
    Midnight doesn't matter—
the heart never closes,
always open to all travelers.

This heart is somewhere in between,
    or both, at parallel times,
        beginnings and endings
            occurring at the same strike of the clock.
    Somebody coming or going, in the same flesh
    on the same legs.

My heart longs to be a family cottage
    with a hearth always burning.
    A wife baking bread, a husband whittling wood
        at the kitchen table.
        A place where people
        actually stay.

We Have Always Been

       Born in the silence,
knit within an ancient explosion,
              spinning
atoms together, forming
molecules,
      held together by who-knows-what.
We're eternal.
I've loved you since
the last time Brahma blinked,
as he sat serenely upon lotus leaves.
This love has traveled lightyears,
from molecule
      to atom joining together,
           from star to starburst to planet to comet,
     to the moon, the ocean, the land.
To me, to you.
     And now we stand here
     at the edge of existence, holding hands.
I know we have always existed,
and we always will
     in one form or another,
but in this right-here moment,
     let's you and I just continue to be.

We Got

We got
        oohs and ahs,
things we do in the dark.
           We got
sighs, moans, cries, groans.
We got
        sweat, we got
wet, we got hard.
        We got love,
              lust,
              aches,
              and pains.
You hurt so good.
        Shaking thighs,
        hard-pressed fingertips,
            lingering tongues.
We got
        yes, no, maybe tomorrow.
        We got
tonight, for sure.
        Right now,
you got
        my legs in the air.
           I got
your tongue in my mouth,
        your lips everywhere.
 You got
        your hands on my hips,
that
        pull, push, pull, push magic.
We make
        something outta nothing—
sweat, saliva, lust, trust.
        Come with me,
because all we got
        is now.

Princess Charming

These fairy tales are some of the biggest reasons I am the way I am.
I've slept upon cinders for years,
yet no magic-slipper-carrying,
poverty-overlooking prince has ever crossed my path—
charming or otherwise.
I've been asleep far too long,
my lips frozen together, my eyes closed.
For centuries, I've been frozen in time,
waiting,
waiting, waiting
for a beautiful, sensitive, understanding
figment of the collective imagination.
I spent years trying to be still,
to wait for a rescuer, someone
to take me from this life
instead of finding myself.
Opening wide as a flower does
yet without the benefit of sun's rays.
Women like us, we weave gold,
take tea with our godmothers,
try to mine our gems while unequipped
with the right tools.
We give up our legs, our tongues.
We have no voices.
We want to be seen,
forgetting all along (if we were ever taught
in the first place),
                    that we were here to begin with.

3 A.M.

It's 3 a.m.
    and I'm thinking of you,
        how home seems to move on two legs,
        and how peace manifests
    from booming laughter
    pushed forth from lungs
        surrounding
one of the kindest hearts I've ever known.
    It's 4 a.m.
        and I'm awake, remembering
        how your hands would cradle me,
            delivering a new woman,
                soaked in the fluids of possibility,
        drenched in optimism
        and your care.
            It's 5 a.m.
                and I can feel your lips on mine,
                a dull pain, sort of phantom
limb.
    I ache, and there's no relief
        except your voice in my ear,
        your hands on my hips,
            your legs tangled in mine.
                It's 6 a.m.
The sun rises,
    its rays far-flung across the ceiling
    into the corners of my room.
        I realize again you are not here.

    The morning has arrived too soon—
        too soon.

Malnourished

There's no passion here,
just warmed-over convenience.
Excitement's been left in the freezer,
and I'm left with
factory-processed junk food kind of love.

>That Swanson's peas in the potatoes
>with apple dessert
>kind of love.

>>That swing by the drive-thru on the way to somewhere,
>>gobble in the car on the way

with a five-course meal in mind kind of love.

That disappointing, limp fry kind of love, that smashed burger
that don't look like the commercial infatuation.
This food isn't filling.

>Looking for soul food love—

>>Grandma's black-eyed peas,
>>collard greens, neck bones,
>>hot water, cornbread, peach cobbler
>>kind of love.

That satiation to the toes, that itis kind of love.
Want to fall asleep because I'm so satisfied love.

>And so,
>I hit reverse in the driveway, because
>even though I'm hungry,
>til I get what I need,
>I guess I'm just gonna have to starve
>on ideas of being full,
>because an empty stomach is better
>than settling for empty calories.
>It might be better to leave space
>for something more filling.

Carl Takes Dolly Out to Taco Bell in Their RV

What a man! What type of man
        stares into the sun, lets a star
be flesh and blood,
              does not ask her to dim her light
or to stop stealing the oxygen
        from the air on a Taco Tuesday?

What kind of man
        gives her space to be simple,
        American, on a late night
        craving a bean burrito or perhaps
        a double-decker taco with an inner
        cheesy taco shell, to sip her
        frozen Baja Blast
        and eat some damn cinnamon twists—
or maybe she'd order an Enchirito
if she so chooses?

How normal, how endearing, how sexy.

No wonder they've been married
57 years. In a world of haters
and groupies, he's just a man,

ready to whip the old RV
into the local Taco Bell lot,
run in, pick up the order,
              nurture the divinity he's privy to,
        and continue to let her be regular—
        no judgment if she only wants
mild sauce with more onions
but no Diablo sauce
because she's a devout
Christian, forever and ever
                    amen.

Could Be

I could be a syrupy,
sticky-sweet sensation
in the back of your mouth,
leaving sugar residue.
I could be a warm wind
whispering from the dark,
encouraging mayhem.
I could be a fantasy,
all by myself,
turn me on,
all by myself.
Baby-soft, thick thighs
by myself.
I could be
a brazen hussy or a lady.
I could be
a stranger or a twenty-year lover.
I could be
someone you might take home to Mama.
I could be the one you bend over
in her laundry room.
Nice as can be, naughty as all get-out.
Virgin or whore I could be,
split down the middle,
a changing face—
kind of like Hecate.
I could be
any and all those things,
depending
on how you decide
to decipher the mystery
of my honey.
Something out of your wildest dreams,
something other than what I seem.
Ain't no telling
all that I could be.

True Satisfaction

He told me
        there's no way to satisfy him.
Doesn't matter how long you try.
His stamina: legendary.
Sounded good,
sounded like all the men
who spit game throughout history.
                              I should know—I've heard them all.
                                I come from something timeless.
I thought
maybe this time could be "challenge accepted."
Someday.
Yet another notch
on my belt of men
who talked up their skills
but lacked execution
against these ancestral curves and waves.
        Most men drown
or careen off my cliffs,
meeting an untimely end,
their boasts dying in their throat,
their last breaths
sounding like moans—
        then silence.
A disappointed quiet,
then a squeak
because he's exhausted
and afraid.
A shuffle out the door,
                      a name added to the list of men to tune out
                                        forever.

Summer '13

We weren't gods,
    though we tore up the countryside
    and down the shore,
    tucking our feet into hot sand,
    roasting our toes like cassavas,
yams, plantains.

It was a simple life.
    Me, so hard to please,
    you, rich in belly laughs
    and strong hands
    and a third-world
    motorcycle.

I was so different then,
    recovering from broken
and cold in my flesh. Unthawing,
    you came and whispered
    my name, hot.

We aren't gods.
        The cracks started to show.
        We, enamored with the divinity
        in each other's eyes.

We found it was lust.

Today, I'm growing a new heart,
        something immortal,
        not subject to tidal waves
        or whims.

Unreachable, protected,
        not left sitting out
        like fruit in a Ghana
        market stand in summer's
        rainy season.

How the flesh of what
we thought was love
fell apart like dirt roads
in a downpour.

Haikus for an Ex-Lover

I torture myself
looking at pictures of you.
It hurts, your absence.

Did we ever love
each other? Was it all a
lie? You'll never tell.

Who was I to think
you could love me, truly? I
was too much for you.

I lie here alone,
missing you, who probably
never was. You lied.

Stuck here writing love,
sick haikus, disillusioned.
Why'd I even try?

I miss the feelings
that untruth wrought, the joy your
lies brought—love 'fore loss.

Again, I lie here,
stuck and brooding, afraid to
love again. Thank you.

Doing Laundry

The long and slow end of a relationship can be like a pile of dirty clothes.
Picture a mound of expectations in a corner,
        soiled by reality and the dust of disappointment,
memories like stains upon the beautiful and vibrant fabrics,
            the scent of potential fading away
to be replaced by the bitter stench of decayed love,
        wrinkled time and hope,
mingled with thoughts of him, which no longer have any place
      in your wardrobe.
The stiff denim, weakened and wrinkled by disappointment
        because he wasn't able (or willing) to be who he said he was.
            Delicate hopes rucked and ripped by circumstance.
            Scratchy wool irritations clogged with dust and static.
Sometimes, it's tempting to let this continue to pile up
and overtake the corner
        where you hid the memories until the mound
becomes a hill becomes a mountain becomes your life,
        and your room gains a permanent stench that permeates
your whole house.
        Then, it becomes time to do laundry.
Break down the mountain of neglect, disappointment, and rage.
         Sort your disillusionments from what good memories you have—
        how, in the beginning, his eyes smiled whenever he saw you.
Wash away the way his mouth twisted near the end
when you tried to place your hand in his.
        How softly his lips caressed your name
        as it left his mouth that first month.
Soak the hardness of his eyes during the last days away in the wash.
        How his fingers tenderly caressed your back
        the first time you made love.
Spin away the cold shoulders, ignored calls, and lack of consideration.
          Dry your tears,
because these loads are no longer your own.
        Slowly, the piles shrink, the rank stench of despair
begins to dissipate, and life begins to make more sense
        as the colors become brighter and your whites get whiter.

The darks haven't faded, which is a good thing.
            Fold and hang up your memories,
              free from the dust of anger and sadness.
Put them away, but save the good times and cloak yourself in them
                (since being naked in public is bad form),
                        and let the bad stuff continue to flow down the drain.

WITH *America*

Pre-K

A little boy fixes his hand
into the shape of a gun,
takes off running,
yelling,
Pow!
Pow!
Pow!
You're dead!
Can barely form the consonants,
no idea what the words mean.

A four-year-old girl fixes her mouth
to call herself stupid,
and no matter how many times I offer
the stem of an affirmation
or give examples of good qualities,
she repeats it.
I can't pull stupid and ugly from her hands,
prune the weeds sprouting there already.
Her friend joins in,
singing the worst nursery rhymes of terrible things.

A child sits under the jungle gym,
watching,
waiting,
a pair of eyes in new flesh.
Among the dirt, a fresh soul
sits. What has he seen yet?

Another young boy fixes his blocks
into a semi-automatic.
The biggest one in the world,
he says.
The biggest ever.
A multicolored monstrosity
of plastic and intent.

Who taught them? Who will?

Capitol

I) My ancestors sit on each of my shoulders,
   screaming, crying 400-year-old tears.

II) Nobody's learned a damn thing,
    yet they gave themselves credit,
       somehow surprised
       we're failing.

III) They should never call us monkeys again.
     They're the ones who threw shit
     in the halls they call sacred.

IV) This is a beast, feasting on 400
    years of red meat, hate, ignorance,
    entitlement. Jim Crow dances
    on all of our graves.

V) There's your truth and there's the truth—
   and wisdom knows the difference.
   Courage walks forward when correct.

VI) They arrested the usurpers later. Let them
    go home after beating and tasing protectors,
    after inhaling bear mace. Let them leave
    whole-bodied, picking shreds of clues
    from their bragging. Called them patriots
    with no sense or sound of irony.

VII) Maybe no one else smells the hypocrisy.

Black-Girl Blood

Black-girl blood don't hit the same,
don't flow the same.
Our breaths ain't as urgent.
We beg and we beg,
beg you not to hurt us.
Beg you to hold us delicately—
we're also fine china,
not just animals with fine vaginas.
My foremothers were forced to do things like
have babies in between waving rows of cotton,
locked up in breeding farms,
hidden away, bred like pack mules.
So it's no wonder, centuries later,
you're still confused.
You rely on our strength
because who else could have put up with that
and still stood tall, creating more ripples
in the fabric of time as your babies sucked
my mothers' nipples,
raising America on the milk of the disregarded?
Every time we march, we march for our men,
we march for our fathers, brothers, sons.
We march as if our granny's moms and daughters ain't
stolen away in the dead of night,
after flash-bang, door bust, flashlight beam, battering ram.
In early morning darkness, a light
snuffed too soon, and we don't even find out about it on the news.
Have to wait for hashtags, videos, tears.
Will there be a march in the streets?
Will they light a few candles?
I ask 'cause Black-girl blood don't hit the same.
If it did, I wouldn't have to beg you to say her name.

Dear Mother

       You made me love you.
You told me, practically since incubation,
I belonged to you because you birthed
me. I remember every morning, standing
pigeon-toed, my brown hand over my heart,
unwaveringly pledging my allegiance to you.
       My brown eyes raised in faith
because I just knew you would never betray or hurt me.

Around the age of six, when my mother was in the Navy,
my hand moved from my heart to my brow. I saluted you.
Years later, I learned you never wanted me.
You considered me a missed abortion, an aberration.
       One day, I learned that your dusky children
           weren't the ideal.
       The winds of history carried the whispers and screams
       of those sacrificed to your American dreams.
The God you swear you believe in knows
I loved you more than three-fifths of a heart's capacity.
I loved you so much I was sick with it,
       wondering why you wouldn't love me back.

I just wanted to belong,
to be held like you hold your other,
more worthy children. Still, sometimes I ache for your arms to protect me.
    Instead, your cold shoulder tenses
      whenever I try to rest my head on it.

           Now, my voice chokes when I even think of singing
    about your majesty, your fairness, your freedom, your glory.
    Of purple mountains, golden grains, and God's grace.
    I can't help but think of twisted faces above noose knots,
    burning crosses, ravaged bodies, and waterlogged goddesses
    left to drown at the bottom of the Atlantic.
Why did you lie to me?
    Would it be bad form to have your child, just-birthed, hate you
    straight from your birth canal?

Here I am, a bastard, waiting for you to acknowledge me,
    yet you continue to turn your face away.
        Deep inside,
a small voice still cries out for you.

    Mother, please love me.
           I have no one else in this world.

Ode to the Mother of a Church Boy

Imagine a mother on Sunday morning, dragging
her son to the shower, making him breakfast
like every Sunday morning.
Cracking eggs into a skillet so he could dip
his toast in the yolk before children's church.

Every Sunday, for years, he grew up
in the church, sang hymns, gave offerings,
took notes in the margins of his Bible.

Imagine thinking you raised a godly son,
taking him to rifle practice, guns
on your bookshelves, empty of actual reading materials.

Imagine one day, that mother's son
deciding false evidence appearing real
justified his snuffing out the lives of those whose eyes
he couldn't see the light of God shining through.
Lights out. Maybe later he'll tell us why.

Imagine a church, erasing her son's well-raised self
from the church rolls, snuffed out like he never existed.

I wonder what they'll say about his background.
Imagine all the questions they'll ask her.

On the Occasion of Robert E. Lee's Statue, Dismantled and Removed 131 Years Later aka "Whose Streets? Our Streets!"

If you give a loser a pen,
he will rewrite the story
into one of his own victory.

    Repeat it long enough, it becomes the truth
    coming out of the mouths of schoolchildren.

Ignorance codified, tested, passed
    on for generations.

        Placed on a pedestal, concrete tough,
        tin wrapped in more precious metal,
        blocking your eyeline
        from what's actually true.

Decades passed. The losers' "victories" shared verbatim.
School boards tremble, sessions interrupted
by these fighting phantoms,
    also known as What Actually Happened.

Critical Race Theory, they call it, red faces
cloaked in tears, mouths wide, spouting lies
they were taught to be true.

They really believed it, too.
    They built a nation
    around a lie and called
    it "Southern Heritage."

        At least once, the monument's face was bathed
        in the light of thousands of tiki torches,
        its metal rang with the echos from lips
        afraid to be displaced. What will they replace
        it with?

Blood stained the asphalt
after an acolyte, so afraid,
pressed gas pedal, ran over
the best of us, all for a lie
that might finally—hopefully soon—
be put to rest. Dismantled,

        like the personhood of African ancestors,
        forcibly removed, like Jackson did
        the Natives, hidden like our shared history.

With its removal, we are again put to the test.
    Will we finally let the untruths die,
    or will the loudest loser continue
    to force our teachers to lie?

What Is America to Me?

Golden grains and purple mountains majesty,
apple pies, and baseball, and liberty—
I ask, what is America to me?
Black-bottom blues, 'cause my love done me wrong.
Can't help but hum the same old song.
Home of the slave and land of the free—
tell me, brother, what's America to me?
Bruising billy clubs and bullets flung,
poplar trees where my people hung.
Can't find any place from sea to shining sea—
Lord, tell me, what's America to me?

What is America to me?
From rock to rock, I roam,
can't possibly think of her as home,
her welcoming arms never shown—
disdain is all I see.
Not my mama—
what is America to me?
Sprung from her loins,
she birthed me, but every day I'm in her presence,

she never ceases to hurt me.
Dashed away like dirt, she abused me.
But when she needed something done,
she always used me, ground me up,
spit my bones from the earth.
As towers fell, slave ships bore them.

Who can tell me,
who can foot the blame
for the blood in the soil, the hands that ceaselessly
picked golden grains?
There's no one to demonstrate
with any lucidity.
Someone, please tell me—
what is America to me?

My country 'tis of thee,
sweet land of hypocrisy,
of thee I sing.
Land where my father hanged,
land of my mother's pain,
reverberating my grandmother's lost name.

Will they ever let freedom ring?

Calling in Black

I had to call in Black today—
        the mask cracked,
        the tone couldn't
        be softened, the effort
        just wasn't there.

Couldn't care enough
to muster the enthusiasm
to step outside of myself
to focus on the minutiae—
        the meetings, the articles,
        the small talk, couldn't do.

So I called out Black today.
        Code-switch machine broke,
        all because another hashtag
        birthed, and I wish I didn't have to
        wish I could be blithe enough
        to expect somebody to care
        about office politics, spreadsheets,
        systems, with no idea or attempt
        to notice the loads carried.

Ignorance is bliss.

        Can't slow down enough
        to temper the tone
        to focus on shit that don't matter
        to ask you to care more
        without
        you calling it "politics."

So I called in Black today
        because it's better that
        than to unleash Black rage in HR.
I chose to rest and come back Monday—
        maybe.

WITH *Sadness*

Birth

As you felt the hands around your neck, pulling

        you into the bondage of existence,
        free.

As your eyes opened to the sun for the first time,

        your lungs flexed, exhaled

                a scream,
                the shock of cold air
                on your skin.

You had no idea

        life could be this hard.

The harshness of a

            SMACK

as the doctor's hand

        slapped against tender skin,

your toothless mouth wide as tears

        fell down your cheeks,
        the first of many.

What is this brand-new reality?

        This pain as they cut the cord,

the last link to home, the tunnel closed.

        You can never return, the warm waters

splashed out—

        you will never swim in them again.

The nurse's warm, analgesic hands swabbed you down
        then wrapped you in swaddling cloth,
free from the blood that heralded your arrival.

        The fear began as your impotent arms
              waved like white flags in the air.

Your first five breaths, that was as good as it would ever get.
      (Except for when they lay you upon your
      mother's breast

for your first sleep after the traumatic awakening.)

      For the rest of your life, you'd dream
of water slides, warm pools, and blood,
            then tell creation myths about great floods.
What is it to be human besides being afraid?
That day of your birth, you laid there,
    safe in your mother's arms, not knowing that life
would never be as good as when you listened to her heartbeat
        for the very first time.

Resentment

She kept her resentment close, like a security blanket.
Could never release the weight long enough to even think of flying.
She let anger coat her lips, a fine film
of rancor. Sharpened her tongue
and used it to pierce holes into
the deepest, softest parts of her fellow man.
She hugged it close like she did her children,
let it rest on her hips, her shoulders.
Couldn't let it go, and it continues to smolder.
If I could, I would release its tentacles from around her,
yet it seems she prefers it surround her.
She
birthed and raised her children with it
as one would with a spouse.
Now she sits watching the evening news
with furrowed brow,
replaying memories on the backs of her eyelids
between blinks, like metroplex screens,
reliving memories and things that cannot (but should be) unseen,
humming that familiar refrain.
Despite the sun's rays, she still prefers to sit in the rain.

S.A.D.

The taste of rain upon the tongue.
The scent of melancholy rising like petrichor
from the dirt beds of my imagination.
I wish for summer sun on my face,
washing against me like waves against the shore,
not these snowflakes falling,
accumulating, burying me in sadness.
What about springtime's optimism?
The flower blooms—blue skies and green life.
The leaves are dead now, just stark gray
skies with branches outstretched
like a hospice patient's fingers grasping
as they gasp the last few breaths of life.
I can only lie here wishing for sunshine
to light the dark corners of this room.
Blues and jazz tunes because
        the winter silence is deafening—
        a cacophony of nothing.
No life and no light, no birds singing, no leaves.
Dance in the breeze.
And I just lie here, wondering if my spring
will ever return.

A Love Story
Dedicated to MJ

I can remember
loving you under blacklight,
your aura. You filled my head with possibilities.
I can remember the first
inhale that October evening,
pulling the lighter from the ember.
You made my head swim—
but, oh, the delicious drowning,
no objection.
I found you and it was good.
2 a.m., throat dry, but
(as loved ones seem to)
you changed,
as did the circumstances.
I ran to you because he happened.
Your arms made sense at the time.
You were my comfort, my rebound,
but now you make my fucking
head hurt, taking away my strength
while making my heartbeat faster.
It's irregular how you offer comfort in one breath,
pain in the next. Inconsistent
in most respects. I'm a wreck.
I used you as a substitute while holding back the years.
I think of you now, holding back my tears,
held down by fears.
I thought I loved you. Pressed my lips to yours
daily, gave you my all. For my own good,
had to push you away.
This is a love story, but I have to let you be,
because if I don't, you'll be the death of me.
Heaven knows, you'll be the death of me.

Pills

I.

Here's to the final decision,
one years in the making,
a final commitment.
You wish it went in the other direction,
toward joy, even though
you'd long forgotten the way there.

II.

To all the horizons unseen,
because you couldn't get the scales
to drop from your eyes.
This is for judgment.

III.

To all the times you've found yourself
lacking—to the wanting,
the hunger,
and the feeling you have no right to be full.

IV.

To happiness.
Your empty hands and chest
echoing with the disturbing voices
of those who have long since
forgotten your name.

V.

Because you didn't realize the difference between
wanting to die and wanting the pain to stop.

VI.

To shivering shoulders and a mind
that wonders when it'll all be over.
To fingers that scratch a hash mark down,
to every dawn and dusk on the wall of your self-imposed
prison cell.

VII.

To fingers with no idea they held the key to unlock the bars.
To wasted potential and opportunity,
downcast eyes and brooding mortality.

VIII.

To your last breath, the light that fades
from eyes that have seen too much
and not enough at the same time.

IX.

To hands arthritic, fingers forgotten,
sensations of being held,
the slackening of phalanges
as the pill bottle slips from your grasp.

X.

To the sound of your breath's final rasp.

Insomnia

What lies do you tell yourself
        in your midnight murmurings?
What cliffs do you jump off,
        leaping from one conclusion to the next?

What dark roads do you walk down?
        What perilous path, full of brambles?
What shadows nip at your heels
        as you stumble, as you shamble?

How far have you come, bleeding
        as you go? What progress down this path
so far from home? What price
        have you paid, choosing to go it alone?
What lies do you tell yourself while
        the birds tweet the dawn, as the sun
rises and the rays meet your eyes,
        burning after yet another sleepless night?

Geode

I was pure until I was broken,
a stone mass, dull, somewhat dirty.

Something like steam, trapped deep
inside, I was whole until I was broken

in half, cracked inside,
beauty lies trapped.

One-night whispers and words unspoken,
I wasn't myself until I was broken.

January day, as an adult—
guess I was chosen. It's

eighteen years later.
I guess I was chosen.

I'm still smoking.
I thought I was whole,

at least until I was broken.
Not snapped in half,

something else instead,
inside, shining

like a mirror made of lead.

Divorce/Bankruptcy, Only $250

It's so strange
how easy it is to dissolve
that which was vowed.

Barely costs anything
        except tenderness,
        self-concept, promises,
        sunk-cost—what a fallacy!

Holding on to that which doesn't work.

Instead, look at the signs,
        green, stabbed into street
        corner grass—only $250
        to quit

Your money, your husband, or your wife.
Only a quarter-stack to start a new life.

This Torn-Up Heart

The tongue is a saber
        battling two ideas:
Tell it like it is
        or be quiet and go along.

Patience says:
        Breathe—
this isn't a fight or flight
situation, not life
or death.
        Niceness isn't just
        for its own sake.

Impatience says:
        That shit is fake!
        Tell them what for and what it is
once, so you don't need to repeat it.
        Show them the map,
        so they know exactly
        where they got you messed up.

Patience sits
        quavering but quiet,
        holding tenuously to my demeanor.
After all that spiritual work
and therapy bills
and quit jobs and relationships
you would think I'd have learned
        by now.

Yet impatience pushes forward to
remind me
        of all the bullies,
        the depression,
        the emotional abuse, sexual assault,
        the historical oppressions.
        Of being paid and heard less.

Of love, because I didn't
        (and don't) deserve to be
        treated that way.

Of all the times I didn't fight back,
    of even more bullies
    waiting in the wings,

of holy anger,
of the need to be resilient.

        This torn-up heart, in which
        both patience and its opposite

            must exist.

To just jump out this chest, the impulse,
    I struggle to resist.

WITH *Poets from the Past*

Reply to the Shepherd

Come live with me and be my love.
We'll float higher than the clouds above,
gossamer castles and wind-drawn moats,
fantastic views and pegasus-led boats.

Come live with me and be my dream.
I swear, these words are all they seem.
These words I speak, no less than truth.
Come fly with me, and dip, and swoop.

Come live with me and share these bills.
Sequestered, we, in bricks and steel.
A pull-out couch if you sign your name—
abide with me, our address the same.

I Do Not Believe in Heaven
After E. Dickinson

I do not believe in heaven,

for why waste this precious today

on an unproven, unfulfilled promise

when I have these wings to fly

or legs to walk, to explore my world?

A life to build, hands to touch, eyes with which to see,

sunrise, air to breathe, love to give,

and joyous things to be?

No, I don't believe in angels

with golden harps on high

nor gates through which I must beg admittance.

My heaven is here, its pittance my riches.

Variation on a Theme for English B.
(Or, First-World Problems)

My task tonight is to write a page—
better yet, two.
My professor told me to keep it all.
She said,

    "Let the text come out of you.
      Then it will be true."

I don't know if it will ever be that simple.
Could I ever do justice to the rays of sun
breaking the clouds at the right moment?
A sip of water as it slides down a gullet
the texture of sandpaper?
    Could I express correctly the relief
of finally being heard,

    of having just the right words?

Because folks are dying out here.
Not because of

    missing iPod firmware,
    traffic,
    lack of ergonomic chairs,
    a crashed hard drive.

I often find myself

    at bus stops or
    waiting for trains,
    looking down at my feet as I walk

around, trying to find home
    or any place at all.
I was born near where waves and dreams crash,

    brown- and red-skinned,
    broad-nosed,
    stout of body,

      taking up more space than the world would allow,

living a Rocky Mountain high,
exploring my lows.

      Lost, a pebble

among counterfeit boulders.
Trying to make sense of a universe full of stars
with empty spaces

      and unanswerable questions deep in the heart

of the mess.

      I am an American now,

but I carry the weight of my ancestors in my very bone marrow,

      and I refuse to be ashamed.

My thoughts coil as densely as the very hairs

      on my head.

In my hands, a future cobbled together with wishes,
spit, and masking tape—

      so fragile,

it breaks every morning I wake up,
only to resurrect with dreams and the evening dew.
It's tough, being a machine with no instruction manual,
with no hand to hold

      or light with which to see,

without any clue or guidance on how to live

      and be

without destroying the world further
and inadvertently infringing upon others' right to be free.

This is my page for English B.

Bodies

He said,
        I like my body when it is with your body.
I imagine the friction between two skins
could ignite the world
        like a match against flint
and tinder.
        I like my body when it is with his body.
Fresh and new, he
            reads my skin like the blind
read braille, scars and stretch marks,
                      lines upon which he writes me sonnets.
Skin soft, expectations rough,
            this thin skin, masquerading as tough.
These bodies, intimate under the cover of midnight.
            We share secrets that can only sit in the darkest corners
of attics, our antics. We
            curl around ourselves like cursive.
Bent and distorted, we are beams of light.
        These arms no longer feel like my own.
These legs
        yearn to flex around his waist,
mine enclosed within his hands.
        I said, I like my body when it is with your body,
as musical as the wind whistling through canyons.
        Wrapped in your arms
is the greatest present.

Dear Langston

I wonder if you ever imagined
how your seeds would be planted,
how they'd be watered by the rivers you'd seen.
I remember when I first heard
you wonder about dreams
that are forced to hold too long.
I wonder if you knew how strong
you were,
dear Langston.
I wonder if, wherever you are,
there's a crystal staircase.
I wonder if you ever got a chance to feel like a man,
instead of just some boy.
I wonder if you now know what it's like to feel joy
or if you feel what I someday hope to know.
Dear Langston,
are you happy? Do you eat well?
Have you seen what we've done,
how much further we have to go?
We no longer avert our eyes when they pass,
no longer forced to step our Sunday shoes in mud
so that sidewalks can be clear.
No, we are the dreams you bespoke—
we are America's children,
yet we still have far to go.
Hopefully, we won't dry up and crust over with
sugary cover.
We've come so far, but our struggle is far from over,
dear Langston.

WITH *Writing as a Practice*

Here's a Toast to Unknown Poets

Never venerated, never felt a laurel wreath on their brows,
never heard their names whispered in Ivy League
classrooms—this one's for you.

The ones who sat alone in corners,
frowning,
concentrating,
living,
writing—
this poem is for you.

You, poets, mighty lions of souls
who will never die.
You, ancient griots ,
gods (and goddesses) of syntax and rhyme,
who touch us with a whisper through
reason, experience, and time—
this is a toast to you.

To those who never dreamed their words would inspire,
to the ones who let their lights go brighter and brighter.
Here's to the mad ones, the short ones, the poor ones,
the fat ones,
the loud ones, the quiet ones, the sad ones,
the dreamers, the insomniacs, the screamers,
the ones who lived lives of temperance.
To the ones who sacrificed their souls to their demons—
this is for you.

Did you know your triumphs would keep a young girl
alive someday?

How could you know the shavings of your existence would
fertilize this orchid, the hidden essence of you
found randomly in the backstacks of a college library?

No one ever knows how they will touch a life
until the deeds are done,
placed in the larger context of time,
counted and figured on some sort of grand
accounting sheet.

I wrote you this, a libation for your souls.
This is a toast to the unknown poets
whose stories are rarely told.

Horror Show

A writer not writing becomes a monster,
scarier than anything
scribbled in a notebook.

Can't sleep, pacing
back and forth under low lights
at 2 a.m.,
mimicking the way the pen dances 'cross
blue-lined, blank pages,
holding old manuscripts tight to chest,
closer than a crushed child.

No air, no exposure,
a cloying fear
transforming into a vengeful god,
crumpling existence to toss in the trash bin
over and over again,
Jack Torrance striking the bathroom door with an undull axe.

A writer not writing is full of ideas,
tightly packed like a commuter train at rush hour,
unsafe and underprepared for sudden stops and starts,

tumbling over themselves, over and over,
breaking sanity and restraint.

Looking out of the window
into the tricky-eyed reflection,
mirroring an uncanny valley,
a tilting world speeding, controlled chaos
resulting in a ringing head.

A writer not writing runs away from themselves
toward everything else except a quiet
moment, desk, chair, pad, pen—
the only antidote that will change them back
to something beautiful and true.

Ill

I've got the sickness,
and nothing is a remedy
except verses.
Unscripted, unrehearsed,
not shiny, happy pills
for shiny, happy people,
not anything that can be bought
with money.
Each time, simile spit,
metaphor murmured,
analogy analyzed,
I get somewhat high,
somewhat re-energized
to the point that I
can keep
shoveling bullshit knee-deep,
continue being the lone soldier
in the regiment of me.
Atlas holding my world on my
shoulders,
maybe.
Folks like me understand
this life is
nothing like *Cheers*,
and everywhere we go,
no one but no one knows our name.

I've got the sickness,
and sometimes Langston Hughes,
Dickinson,
Donny Hathaway,
are the only MDs who can
sign the prescription
for various aids to feed my
addiction.
(There's no substitute for
good poetry.)
For instance, the soul lifts
up over this losing battle
on this darkened battlefield,
some light shed, an
indication of the same at
the end of the
tunnel, when
words spill out of the mouths of
angels,
and I,
for the moment, am found, brought
to Earth again.
Once pencil points to paper
to produce the final period,
period,
I am sated for the time being.

I Want to Write a Poem

I want to write a poem.
Not just any poem—
a place to rest
the last period, the release,
the exhalation
of a breath held in for way too long.
I want to write a poem.
A lonely poem
with arms open, ready to hold
the pain that doesn't dare
speak its name.
A poem like a hot toddy
after a cold winter's day.
I want to write a graceful poem.
I imagine fingers flexing
while writing, the pencil dancing
over blue lines,
syntax, stutter, step, pasodoble.
Yeah, I want to write a poem like that,
one with nimble feet and agility,
a poem that feels like being held in the arms
of a lover, secure.
I want this poem to hold me,
keep me steady.
I want to write a poem
that's like a bomb shelter,
since the war never seems to end—
protection against slings and arrows
and lonely nights,
against each ache
and against drone strikes.
Yeah,
I want to write a poem.

Out of Your Head

You're thinking too hard—
        get out of your head.
Dive deep into the ink.
Roll around on the pen's
rollerball, round and round,
as you print yourself
        on these white pages
        between these blue lines,
            serene.

Be like water,
shifting.
Not like ice,
stuck and solid.

        Flow onto the floor,
        onto the parchment,
        like the water in the blood
        your heart beats.

            Take one hand off the other.
            Tell your left-brained impulse
            to pull up a stool,
            to sit in the corner,

because it's time to work.
No time for fear.

Black out,
        intoxicate yourself
        on the feelings.

        Then wake up,
        surprised to have birthed
        another episode of
        the heart's human
history.

WITH *the Past*

Drapetomania

I've seen oceans
in recent memory.
Felt the wind suss
against my cheeks,
whispering,
let go and be free
instead of bound up
in small areas formed tight,
in pain, ravenous,
a raised keloid.
I've seen bright yellow sunshine.
Flowers follow me
like they followed Apollo,
pulling chariots,
welcoming a new day unto humanity.
"Give us us free.
Give us us free,"
and we'll fly away
so gleefully.
But it can't be,
it can't be—
for the thirst for freedom
to them is madness,
you see.

I Am Billie's Gardenia

I sit above her delicate, seashell ear,
    scenting her sickly sweet decay.
I can only do so much
    to stem the progress of her undoing.
Needle marks dot her peanut butter skin,
    giving it the texture of a tangerine,
as rough as her voice when shaped around
    heartbreak.
Her hands, nails chipped, cradle
    the microphone, her eyes closed,
    mouth cavernous, wrists
        still sore from the handcuffs,
    upper arm stiff from the tourniquet.
I wish I could hide her in my folds,
    rebirth her
    so that she could start again.
I love her, but I can't touch her,
    save with scent and saxophone riffs.
The poison floats up the arm
    to the brain,
        and I am no match—
no matter how beautiful—
    for the music she hears when it strikes.
She nods along, nods along,
    nods along...

Enlightenment

Our histories are bathed in blood
as red as the words of Christ.
Imprinted in our memories,
no books.
Everything we owned was perverted,
      stolen,

         burned.

Mass immolation.

We blaze with the passion of those who have lost their names,
desperately trying to find
identity,
lost somewhere in nautical miles,
hegemony,
and lies.
They cut down our pillars,
desecrated our gods,
diluted our bloodstreams,
polluted our water,
stole our land,

and gave us nothing but questions and heartache
in the name of salvation.
History roars
while it disregards our whispers.
For we were considered les gens sans raison,
who worshiped the universe as it stood
rather than what we wished it to be.
Not projecting ourselves into the deepest depths of darkness
or hoping for a deliverer
who considered it a burden
to lighten our "darkness,"
to save us from ourselves,
to "civilize" our wild and unspoiled beauty.

As the bullets   tore through our temples,
            and bombs

we felt our stomachs

drop

as we flew from cliffs,
prayers coating our lips,

without the benefit of
wings,

we realized there was no savior.

For Donny

*On January 13, 1979, at 160 Central Park South,
Donny Hathaway carefully removed the glass from his windowpane,
then jumped fifteen floors to his death.*

On a cold and gray January day,
      you pulled the red curtains back,
      brushed them against the walls
            as you would move a lock of hair behind a lover's ear.
      But there was no one there.
The rain stung your face
      like hornets,
          snow pelted you
      in an effort to step back through the sill
 and disobey your defective and deceptive mind.
      Sometimes I try to imagine
what it's like to soar—
      and then I think of you,
      stepping over the edge,
      sprouting false wings,
         and falling.
Your lips kissing the pavement,
      lips that previously mouthed melodies
      and exhaled harmonies
      that day expelled a death rasp.
I wish I could blame you.
      Sometimes, I feel the curtains calling,
         I see myself falling.
            I think of you and then reconsider.
     I wish you'd thought of your girls and reconsidered,
waited for the day we'd all be free,
         we, so young, gifted, and Black.
            The pavement below your room will never be clean, Donny.
              You believed you could fly, and so you flew.
              You self-destructed, as geniuses often do.

'Trane and Duke

Beloved ancestors,
      come forth from these speakers.
      Let your horn blow, peel, keys
      tinkling.
            Make me feel something again.

The steady rhythm, dependable.
These blues, dispensable.
      As the old tune plays,
      problems become invisible.
            Heart and soul, newly invincible
            when I close my eyes.
      I fantasize sitting in a jazz club
      in front of a glass of brown,
      my body swaying to the 4/4 beat,
      as one does.

Seeing my ancestors alive
      and in their bag,
light glistening on their foreheads
      as their spirits moved.

I see universal love shining through
as I watch 'Trane and Duke
in the midst of my imagined juke.

WITH *the Body*

Wildflower

She searches the mirror daily
for even a glimmer of
beauty.
She is unseen,
unheard,
yet she is still a lady.
Sideways views of herself
yield no satisfaction.
Kisses scars, this, the
only love shown.
This is the only love she knows,
but this is not love
at all.

Each time she rises
from her horrible fall,
she springs up half-heartedly,
because what good is a rose
with a bruised
bloom and no room to grow?
What good is sunshine
when it hides behind clouds of
gray?
Sick of hurting, she closes
and turns her face
away.

Thighs

Walking through crowds,
my thighs make sweet symphonies.

Can't help but sing along,
awkward in the usual silence
between cubicles and the break room.

My pants announce me
down the hall,
but shit, I look good.
These thunder thighs
spark longing in somebody, somewhere.

I don't do this for them.
These thighs
like close columns holding me up.
Heavy like the roof of a Grecian
temple.
Revere the god between these thighs.

Hinted in the scratch
of movement as I announce my coming,
ambling, thighs making
sweet, noisy love
as I walk back to my desk.

I, Too, Sing the Body Electric
(Or, Lady Mag)

They don't speak of the body electric.
It is but a facade, shellacked and coated,
a decoration, not a building to be lived in.
They never mention the sparks of power,
the music made by the mouth,
the legs as they dance along.
They don't sing the body electric,
a body with curves that vary like the mountain peaks
and valleys of the Sierras and Rockies.
The arms that cradle or carry the world
as the need arises.
The eyes that aspire to open as the sun rises,
the laugh lines around the mouth,
the sturdy chin that stays tilted back while dreaming.
They don't believe in the body electric.
They prefer manufactured edifices,
compelled to cut off what offends, change the ugly,
don't embrace it—society demands you erase it.
Fuck your true beauty.
They'll find and debase it
with their cracked mirrors, using the shards to cut away
any confidence.
But I sing the body electric, Photoshop-free.
The strong, sturdy, the ugly and beautiful parts,
and everything that will be.
I, too, sing the body electric,
for the body electric is me.

Shatter

You stare into the mirror,
a shard of yourself,
      wondering if you'll ever surpass
the impulse to vomit at your own reflection.
Nude, you run your fingers over a belly
filled with laughter,
        intuition,
   good food, nutrients,
fats, carbs.
   Your nails scratch, tiny scythes
striking at your self-confidence,
   scarred by circumstance.
Can't bear to believe you are beautiful.
      The mirror shatters.
You are gone. The world does not exist. Memories are all
that remain—
   all the times you forgot yourself
only to remember you are flesh and bone.
Not in debt to random jerkoffs, assholes—
"I don't owe beauty to anyone,"
   and it comes out as a moan.
      You don't owe beauty to the world.
Not here to please anyone but self and those you love,
   those who love you.
      The mirror does not number among them.
Your hands rub softer now, hoping to soothe
   the new scars left by hateful half-moons,
      counting stretch marks as tree rings
because you have dared survive in a Photoshopped world,
   false and demanding.
      Dark marks, gaps between teeth, unruly brows.
   You are beautiful.
      The mirror shatters.
      You are still here.

Forgotten Rhythms

Every month, I phoenix
like so many women—
        identified as a problem,
        less likely to accommodate,
        patience gone, full of ash(e)
        and testosterone.

At any time of the month, they call you
masculine when you get shit done
        stridently, with your voice
        pitched down, unable, unwilling
        to raise it to non-threatening decibels.

The death of the egg—
        why does it
        steal your
        will to live?

                                I guess it figures,
                                  if I gotta go, so do you.
                                  I'll convince you
                                  the world is better off
                                  without you, everybody
                                  hates you, you hate every
                                  body, nothing makes sense,
                                  except all of the above,
                                  and tears,
                                  and chocolate.

Until you see the red,
then it ALL makes sense.

Because, in a way, you just died again,
and it's been that way since you were 12.

Every month you forget—every single one—
one would think that a regularly scheduled
ending would create a rhythm,

*but one would be wrong
apparently.*

After I played Margaret
        and begged God for it
        because I read Judy Blume
                and saw myself, a yearning
        in the main character.

                What a fool you were, a child!

Because every month you find yourself yelling at the sky,
begging your higher self to answer:

                      *Who in the fuck
                      would ever beg
                      for this?*

This Body

Scarred and sacred, this body,
marked with furrows of frustration
like claw marks down a cement wall.
Immovable, this body.
A reflection of the real Venus,
undug from trash heaps millennia deep,
un-thrown from conquest.
This body is a rediscovery,
something I had to learn to find,
a vehicle for a divine mind.
Built for comfort, not speed.
Not a showpiece—lived in
from head to toe.
Once a mystery unknown,
now a daily discovery.
Something has changed.
Not a gut to be grabbed, patted,
wished away.
Not thighs spread sitting,
but centaur-strong, standing tall
and steady to shoot at life's moving targets.
This body is an education,
and I'm working on my diploma.
No CliffsNotes, no map
to truly know the way.
Beauty product marketers
would love me if I didn't fast-forward commercials,
flip past magazine ads,
close my eyes against billboards,
install AdBlock.
This deprogramming is radical—
blocking out the trauma,
all for survival,
all for self-love,
all for the ultimate goal, the seemingly impossible.
Self-love, in this body, is a bloody revolution,

is holy spite,
is ancestor-making,
is a God-given journey.
It fits me like a tailored dress,
like fate, this body,
an expanse of wallflowers,
an interconnected aspen,
a sky full of stars,
a smile in the eye of a child.
This body, uncovered, rediscovered.
This body used to be a battlefield,
a graveyard.
Now it's a fertile field
for all these dreams to grow.

Commonalities

The light gets in/gets out
    through the cracks
        in the armor
        you built up
        after years of pain.

    Became calloused,
    became tough,
    became a crack,
    became rough.
        Burst open
        like a bubble.

Yet beauty exists as if to say,
    look at all this ugly—
    isn't it gorgeous?

Take my hand, and I'll show you
    some of God's creations.
    I'll start by holding up a mirror—
        take a photo to hold you
        on the hardest days.

Because I was born in the dark,
    now I am cloaked in sunrays.

I'll show you that to fail is to succeed,
if only you take away the lesson,
continue to water these seeds

while looking into your eyes,
cause I'm just like you—
    just you in different skin.

WITH *Nature*

Primavera

As the flowers bloom forth in a new spring,
I'm reminded that winter is not the end.

Sing a song of spring
as birds tweet along
and the sun's rays are like spotlights,
highlighting life. Sing a song—

all of us know the tune.
Sing along, sing along,
as mums shake away winter chill,
as cherry blossoms bloom,
as the world awakens and begins again.

Sing a song, for we are alive,
and we dare to open our eyes
to welcome the dawn.

Sing a song—
sing along, sing along,
for we dare to dream... and live.

Earthworm Epiphany

Each movement,
      each piece of flesh
      sinking into soft loam.

      The silence of being alone.

The tight feeling
      of shoulders touching cave walls
      as I inch along
      like an earthworm.

These movements belie
a mission:
      Get to the surface, the sunlight blinding
      the already blind
      but needing the warmth.

Each inching adds inches,
      a hunger
      processing the dirt, making it nutritious
          for any plant that traces
          this path.

      Only way to go is up.

Instinct clenches each muscle
      to grow,
      to make this world better.

Creating the tunnel
      without realizing
      I am the light
          I seek.

Cataclysm

Seems like, sometimes, Earth
is trying to de-people herself,
shake us off her rocks,
flush us from her waters.

She's the rock and the hard place.
Disease after disease,
it's hard to live, so hard to breathe.

Snowstorms all over Texas,
longhorns buried in ice
as if for the first time.

Tornadoes in North Carolina,
degrees subzero,
animals reclaiming.
(Some call it encroachment,
but the animals were here first.)

Humans brought the borders.

The summers see wildfires,
soot flakes, and smudgy skies.
Does Earth think of us as an illness?
Is this her immune response?

We build factories that belch chemicals
and soot, no matter how much
the least of us hate it. Stakeholders
rule. The rich only care if the seeds

grow in their accounts. Yet it gets overgrown,
untouched by these bad decisions.

We talk of removing the undesirables,
never caring enough about human dignity.
Those who pay scientists to lie remain relentless.

Earth cries out, quakes,
molts while we ignore her.

Sometimes, cataclysms don't happen all at once—
this one seems cumulative.

Recalling a Walk Through an Electrical Waste Yard in Ghana, in the Afternoon, Post-Warning

We filed off the bus,
lined up, and warned,
"Don't make too much eye contact
      and watch your step."

We waded down paths through electric
waste, some in flip-flops,
some with toes clad in hiking boots
         and forethought.

With deaf ears,
we passed those who picked through old
computer parts, burned keyboards,
pulled copper wires,
      mining for conflict minerals
      carelessly shipped away
      from first-world problems.

Burning plastic, we held our noses
for five minutes while they stared
at our American clothing, heard
our naive and annoying questions
      with steel lungs and shortened days,
with intuitive understanding.

Although our American tongues needed
translation, we were the real exhibits,
contrary to the tour guide's planning.

The guides told us this walk was to show us
the other side of consumption,
      to let us know how good we have it
      without nuance, with optimism.

We finished our walk as the sun
and heat weighed us down
      like poverty and stolen choices.

We single-filed back onto the bus,
leaving behind a field full of garbage, toxicity,
      and hope.

The Geology of It All

Flying over,
the earth teaches me about layers
      How time gives us rings
        Stratifications and justifications
        Burying ancient happenings
Laid there before any of us
Came flushing out, bathed in birthing fluid

                "All of this used to be underwater, you know"

The sand dunes
The wrinkles caused by persistent streams
And time
So much time

It's easy to forget that life is short
And it's doubly hard to remember
Exactly what that means
Until the debris of daily life covers us

Pressing down
Until our dreams become fossils
Missing organic matter
Become stone
Waiting for us to remember to come back
To dig
To resurrect the living soul
From deep in deserts
With the only clue guiding the way back,
Rivulets in the soil
Caused by wayward tears

I hope you never forget
Again what it all means
The grand scheme of things
Flying over snow-cloaked mountains
I pray you learn to stay above it all
At least sometimes

This ground was once full of life,
Of behemoths, who would swim and dive deep
Now it's all empty land, in which ancient life sleeps and dreams seep.

WITH *My Higher Self*

Nefertiti

Rubies, gold, and silver,
hidden treasures that peek
around corners, only seen
when the light hits
in just the right way.

A deposed pharaoh, forgotten
face of a forgotten people. Still
majestic, still inspiring awe.

Millenia later. Covered with flowers
and dusty. Treasure still glints,
peeks out at you, if you dare to notice.

Covered by cosmetics, these jewels
could shine less. True.
You just have to look a bit harder.

She's still a bountiful bouquet
in an unlikely desert. A crown
jewel for an absent kingdom.

Faceless, full of facets. Diamonds
and rubies. Silver and gold.

Never just Black or ever just white.
She is a style, a way of being.
Untold, hidden. Numinous,
too much for two hands or two
eyes to behold.

Yellow, Forever

I'd be a rhyming poet
writing up a storm, soaking
all who hear these words with wisdom.

I'm sunshine, I'm eternity,
forever intricate eternally,
spitting it, being grit,

living life like I'm a hit.

Trying to be sunshine
opposite shadow—wide pool
of gold, unshallow.

Don't hate my words or swallow.

Let me remind you,
like the sun, the higher self
will come out tomorrow,

flashy like a full-spectrum rainbow,
shining powerful

and yellow
forever.

Maybelline

Every night she looks
in her mirror,
squinting,
applying just the right amount
of blush, eyes shadowy,
peering into herself
to find the good,
to splash it on her lips.
Sipping sweet waters,
her tears flow like her rivers,
shivering at the thought
of being seen for once,
given the ability to choose
for once.
To belong, to walk the path
her high-heels
were made for,
reminiscing about Easy-Bake
Ovens, quick cuisine,
and joy that lasts longer
than the three minutes
it took for the brownies to bake.

Maybe it's not Maybelline,
cause she was always born with it.
Since then, it seems she's been
looking
for one who deserves her best,
but these dudes, man,
with them, it's always a test.
Up on that barstool, she rests,
waiting for the eye contact
that signals
anything but a poison apple.
But, princess, you were always
charming,
awakening at dawn,
birds singing and bells chiming,
winds whispering your name,
bidding you to peer at the sky
when the moon is high
and realize the stars
in your eyes.

Woman
For Kali

"I will dance apart
the universe if you test me."
Eyes a deep sky in mid-winter,
starless, infinite,
spitting one thousand tongues.
Skin, the richest soil.
I've got rivers and miles to go,
so far from home.
I spread my fingers,
knit the world into being
from bone fragments
and whispered names,
from long-dead ancestors stirring
in my veins.
Don't you know I'm not from here?
Maybe
I was stitched together,
whole cloth, sent
on a mystery vessel
lightyears away, or
maybe a wormhole dumped
me into this dimension.
I don't know—
I'm making my way,
I guess.
If I knew how to return, maybe
I'd be there.
It depends on the day,
the minute, the hour.
I'm still learning to stay steady
in the face
of these cosmic winds.
A goddess remaking
at sunrise, morning dew.
Each day, something new.
Awakening, seeing skies so blue,
and I'm like the sun—
sometimes I sink,
sometimes I float,
sometimes I shine.

The Real Me, I've Found

"Seek out that particular mental attribute which makes you feel most deeply and vitally alive, along with which comes the inner voice which says, this is the real me, and when you have found that attitude, follow it."
—William James

This is the real me, I've found—
the attitude to follow. Uncloaked
by ancestral voices.
        The creaky sounds of systems

        created for those before me
        without choices.

I am creating a new thing, more free
than I've ever been to turn around
and reclaim what already belongs to me.
Natural talents, dreams, and abilities.

Seeing butterflies passing by
makes me feel so alive. My inner voice sings
and rhymes with the wind—the tone
and melody, the harmony.
I'm working on creating the dance routine for it
every single day.

It's Time You Spoke

It's time for you to come forward,
to let your voice trumpet.
Trombone your hopes, let your voice
be an orchestra.
Take your time. Enunciate.
Save yourself from the ghosts
    who sit between your ears
        and behind your eyes.
            The ones who didn't question
        when you learned the lies.

One day, somebody told you. Somebody
persuaded you to listen by holding your hands
over her lips.

Somebody had to be there to listen.
Blank, no tape used. The recorder was ready
to spit back what it had been fed.

Release your own voice. Let the vocal tones
escape. It's time for some new music.
Time to pop in a new tape.

Fury (For My Voice)

I'd spit flames if my mouth could push my voice forth,
heating everything, burning those judgments
to ash.
I will toss them in a bonfire, one spreading
from my toes. First, I'll pulverize them
like herbs, grasses, oils, into something
therapeutic, a salve for my thoughts.
A honeyed thing to ease its way back
up when necessary.

> *I only listened because I trusted you more than I knew*
> *how to trust myself. Now I must dust myself off,*
> *sluice off the mud.*
> *Travel upward from the lungs*
> *to the air outside my face, this voice.*
>
> I'd give anything to share my voice.

Pebbles

Pebble 1

I set down my small self
    like a dark, round pebble
    on the side of the road
    to be kicked along
    somewhere else.

Before I did,
    I rolled it around
    in my fingertips,
    savoring its prior
    usefulness, its
    protection, its
    steadiness.

I've outgrown it.
    My hands now hold
    much bigger things,
        like other hands,
        worlds, words,
        wealth. Higher
        self on a higher
        vibe. Dreams,
        aspirations, and
        inspirations. Spare
        breaths, genius,
        and pens to write
        the revolution.

I set it down and picked up peace instead.

Pebble 2

No self-concept.
No cubicles.

No khakis.
No performance reviews.
No decorations.
No expectations.
No questions.
No answers.
No hindrances.
No poisons.
No love.
No frustrations.
No material possessions.
Nobody to impress.
No one to disappoint.
No space to hold anything in my hand
      except the small space
       left for peace.

Pebble 3

Smooth stone printed blue,
a peace and alien form in
this trembling hand.

Pebble 4

I release these expectations,
though they fly back into my palms
as soon as I'm unaware.
I toss this pebble across a river,
skipping only to sink to the bottom,
leaving my heart and hand empty.

At least until I decide to roll peace
around and over my knuckles
like a quarter, a down payment
on my freedom.

Pebble 5

Feels like the will to control,
unyielding, unwieldy.
I am as small as this pebble
after dreaming of myself as a boulder.
I had to awake,
as my tears eroded my illusion.
Peace comes as the trouble dissolves
in the face of hot weeping. Without
the capacity to control, I'd rather be sleeping.

Pebble 6

It's either let go or be dragged.

Fault Lines—Blessings to Self and Others

Every morning, I wake up,
        bake up,
          groggy because I stayed up.
          I'm laid up,

    reading the news until
    my heart breaks.
    Spend a couple of hours
    on my mistakes.

        I'm from the land of oceans
        and earthquakes,

        bad examples
        and heartaches,
        late-night sins
        and early wakes.

I reflect on it, day to day.

Wake up every morning
with heartache
because my whole life,
I thought I was a mistake.

Told my mama, she don't regret what God made.
Only said hallelujah til her teeth ached.

She told me,
    "You been a blessing since the womb,
and it will be that way til the tomb."

The Directive

In the darkness behind these eyelids,
in this mind, the only sign above, bright red
glowing—HEAL
        as livid as a wound.

HEAL, transmute, for the good of the world—
        if I have to be here, in this place,
might as well heal,
        show my sisters I can
        send healing and care
        back seven generations.
Plant seeds for trees I'll never see,
        seven generations forward.

Heal, even though it isn't easy,
        become potent medicine
        for those who need it,
seal hearts, love, and love
        until it feels awkward.

Speak the truth and the truths of your mothers
who wouldn't have dared
        at the threat of a noose.

HEAL—call the nervous system
        out of surviving
        and into thriving.

Regulate and fail forward. We're all walking
        these baby steps together.

Got my ancestors in me, living
        from my eyesight,
        especially at midnight
        when the veil is thin,
                I hear a quiet voice whispering,

        Well done, daughter. Well done.

www.ingramcontent.com/pod-product-compliance
Lightning Source LLC
Chambersburg PA
CBHW070105080526
44586CB00013B/1192